Building Dikes and Levees

Nancy Anderson

Rosen REAL READERS

Rosen Classroom™
New York

Many people live near rivers, lakes, and oceans. What happens if they flood? The water can cause a lot of harm to buildings, homes, and farms!

People build dikes to stop floods. Dikes are walls along the water. They keep water from flooding land. They keep water levels safe.

Some dikes are made naturally. Soil gets pushed up to the sides of a river. This is nature's way of stopping a flood.

Sometimes people need to build dikes. They can use concrete blocks. They can also use big rocks.

Heavy rains start to fall. The river starts to get higher. People run outside to fill sandbags. They stack the bags along the river like a wall.

The water rises, but the dike holds it back. It sends the water down the river. The water does not flood the area.

Sometimes construction crews build dikes. They use big machines like bulldozers to move soil close to the water. They make a long and high wall with the soil.

Sometimes a river is too narrow. To stop flooding, construction crews make it wider. The wider a river is, the more water it can hold.

Dikes are common in the Netherlands. "Dike" is a Dutch word that means the bank of a body of water. In America, dikes are also called levees.

Dikes can help create farmland. They can also keep rivers, lakes, and oceans from flooding. Dikes help shape the land!

Glossary

bulldozer A large, powerful tractor that is used for moving dirt and rocks.

concrete A strong building material made of broken stone, sand, cement, and water.

flood When a large amount of water covers an area of land that is usually dry.

sandbag A bag filled with sand that is used to build walls against rising water.